Crúachan, Co. Roscommon, the sacred royal assembly site of
Connacht, named after Crochain Croidhearg, who fell to earth from
the lap of the sun goddess Étain and lives nearby in Oweynagat cave,
which is penetrated by sunlight at midsummer dawn.

First published 2008 AD
© Wooden Books Ltd 2008 AD

Published by Wooden Books Ltd.
8A Market Place, Glastonbury, Somerset

Cataloguing in Publication Data
McDonnell, H.
Ireland's Holy Hills & Pagan Places

A CIP catalogue record for this little book
may be available from the British Library.

ISBN 978 1 904263 62 3

Recycled materials throughout.

Printed and bound in Europe
by The Cromwell Press, Wiltshire.
100% recycled papers by Paperback.

IRELAND'S
HOLY HILLS &
PAGAN PLACES

by

Hector McDonnell

To Nelson, whose kindness and help has been a constant support.

The illustrations are mainly taken from The Scenery and Antiquities of Ireland illustrated by W. H. Bartlett, pub. London, circa 1850; Antiquities of Ireland by E. Ledwich, pub. Dublin, 1804; and Early Christian Architecture in Ireland, by Margaret Stokes, pub. London, 1878.

Skirk Henge, Co. Laois, 'a pagan shrine on a lofty hill where the eye has an extensive range ... surrounded by a deep intrenchement, and within is a pyramidical stone six feet high.' (from Ledwich, Antiquities of Ireland).

CONTENTS

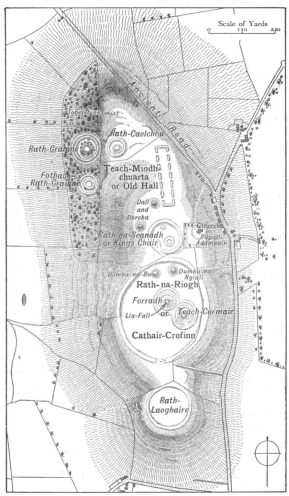

An early attempt to relate the visible structures of Tara to legendary names.

INTRODUCTION

Ireland has an extraordinary wealth of mythological material, and almost every hill, mountain, river, valley and lake has legends attached to them. Many of these tales come out of very ancient lore. Some even claim to name the first settlers, saying where they came from, where they landed and what happened to them. The medieval Lebor Gabála Erenn, the Book of Invasions, is a major source for this material, and much spin doctoring went into its creation.

The Iron Age Celts, arriving thousands of years after the first settlers, reworked the country's ancient mythologies, so as to amalgamate them with their own, and thus created a new brand of Irish legend. Much later still, medieval churchmen gathered together all the traditions they could about tribal origins, concocted biblically slanted versions, and created a genealogical framework to the myths that would conveniently lead back to Noah and Adam. To achieve this neatly they made almost everyone descend from a Spanish prince called Míl who himself descended from Scota, a daughter of an Egyptian pharaoh called Níl, Noah's great-great-grandson.

They even managed to give Tara's pagan, and very phallic, inauguration stone, the Lia Fáil, a respectable biblical origin as Jacob's Pillow, which Míl's family had conveniently brought with them.

Puffin Hole near Kilkee, Co. Clare. Cuchulain leapt between similar rocks not far away at Loop Head.

J. T. Willmore

Nothing Lost
the First live on

The Lebor Gabála Erenn relates that Noah's grand-daughter Cesair brought Ireland's first settlers to Dingle. Only one survived, for five thousand years, sometimes as a fish or bird, and so saw the next lot land with Parthalán in Mayo. Their line also ended, in a plague.

After that came Nemhedh. His wife, goddess Macha, lived on Ard Macha (Armagh) while Nemhedh cleared twelve plains for farming, lit the first fire at Uisneach, Ireland's sacred centre, and drove some demonic giants called the Fomhóire away to the west. His people then fled, but five, the Fír Bolg brothers, returned to split Ireland between them.

Later, the Tuatha Dé Danann arrived, the tribe of the deities Anu and the Daghdha. They were metal workers. A magic cloud landed them at Lough Corrib and Sliabh an Iarann, the Iron Mountain, with magical tools: the Lia Fáil, Lugh's spear, Nuadha's sword and the Daghdha's cauldron. They drove the Fír Bolg to the country's western edges, but their kingship then fell to Lugh, a Celtic god described here as the Fomhóire king's grandson.

Some time afterwards Míl's sons landed in Kerry. They threw back the Tuatha Dé Danann, finally forcing them to abandon this world and become underworld gods, with their homes inside the country's hills and megalithic sites.

Above: Bantry Bay. The south-western coast's hills and bays remember many ancient invasions. here the French attempted one in 1796, while in the far distance is Mount Gabriel, home to the archangel and also to some very early Bronze Age copper mines. Below: Early Irish metalwork. Arrow-heads, spear-tips and a cauldron.

CREATION OF THE SACRED
shaping the beyond

Ireland's early inhabitants frequently expressed their sense of awe in stone monuments. The simplest, though not the oldest, are standing stones, which a medieval poem said marked heroes' graves. Other beliefs persist. One Ulster stone bears a harvest god's name, some have holes used in fertility or oath taking rituals, and others are petrified individuals. Many, chosen for their dramatic weathering, are strangely shaped or scored with grooves.

The bronze-age Irish created hundreds of stone circles and typically buried their dead in stone cists, while their neolithic predecessors preferred megalithic structures: including portal dolmens, court cairns and passage graves with inner womb-like chambers, all created with impressively large stones, and covered by large cairns. Fires were often lit at their entrances, they usually contained ashes of the dead, and were sited on commanding positions.

Drombeg stone circle, Co. Cork

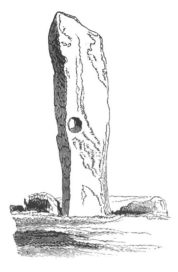

Left: Doagh Stone, Co. Antrim.
Couples pledged their troth by
clasping hands through the hole.

Below: New Grange, Brú na Bóinne,
one of the greatest megalithic sites, is
roofed with flat stones and corbelling.
Stone bowls which held human
ashes stand in recesses, elaborate
patterns are incised on particular
stones and a 'roof box' (a window
over the entrance) is aligned to
capture light from midwinter sunrise.
Well- worked bone pins or smoothed
beads, ceremonial tools, stone balls
and phalluses have all been found
in these Stone Age monuments, the
shrines, mausoleums and cathedrals
of their day.

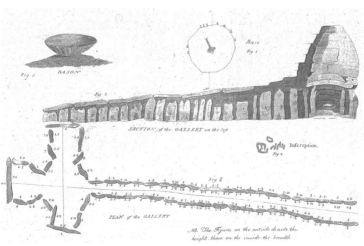

Fig 5 — BASON

Base Fig 1

SECTION of the GALLERY on the left

Inscription. *Fig 4*

Fig 2

PLAN of the GALLERY

NB. The Figures on the outside denote the
height, those on the inside the breadth.

Skies in the Landscape
holding the heavens

The earliest megalithic monuments are possibly as early as 5,000 BC, at Carrowmore, Sligo, predating Irish agriculture. Two millennia later beside the river Boyne arose Brú na Bóinne, the feasting hall of Bóinn, the White Cow goddess, who straddles earth and heaven, letting her Milky Way flow across the night sky while her river enriches the earth.

This river-star myth must have been a widely held Palaeolithic concept, for the Egyptian goddess Nut also arches the sky, with both the Milky Way and the Nile's floods issuing from her, and other versions occur in India, China and the Americas, as is also the case with the Great Bear constellation myth.

Seasonal events were clearly celebrated, as the monuments are often aligned towards dawns and sunsets of midsummer, midwinter and the equinoxes, and they appear to make a network of interrelated sites. A Knowth passage looks to Loughcrew, where others point to Tara in Meath, and Carrowmore and Carrowkeel in Sligo, while Tara's also look north to Slieve Gullion and south to the Wicklow hills, whence came Brú na Bóinne's glittering quartz.

This Stone Age awe of the heavens also colours the myths. Crúachan, Connacht's assembly hill is named after Crochain Croidhearg, who fell from her mother the sun goddess's apron and lives in Oweynagat cave, which opens to midsummer dawn.

Above: Looking west at Tara towards Loughcrew. Below: The entrance to New Grange, Brú na Bóinne, as it was before excavation and reconstruction.

ENCASING TIME
marking seasons

The Irish megalithic builders effectively created sacred caves or portals to spirit realms, related them to seasonal events, and incised stones with geometric designs inspired by the 'entoptic' phenomena seen in shaman trances in all neolithic cultures.

At midwinter dawn and sunset, Brú na Bóinne and Dowth let sunlight into deep interior places, while Knowth opens to equinoxes and also the northern moonrises of its 18 year cycle, when moonlight touches representations of its phases and face. Others have equally well conceived alignments. The largest of Loughcrew's thirty passage cairns has a highly decorated stone in its chamber which is bathed by the equinoctial sun, and Carrowkeel's biggest cairn lets midsummer sunsets enter by a 'roof box', just as New Grange's roof box brings in midwinter dawn.

Myths describe the most elemental powers at work within these shrines: the father-sun god, the Daghdha, enters Brú na Bóinne to impregnate the sky-cow-river goddess, Bóinn, and Slieve Gullion's passage cairn is Cailleach Bhéarra's house, a harvest goddess who changes from aged hag to young girl and lures young men into her depths. This cairn points south to Cailleach Bhéarra's other hill, Loughcrew.

Many Irish festivals mark this magic calendar: Lughnasa is remembered in late summer fairs, Samhain in Halloween, the winter solstice in Christmas, Beltaine in May Day festivities, the vernal equinox with St Patrick and Oímelg with St Bridget's Day.

Left: The east recess at New Grange, Brú na Bóinne. The eastern recesses are generally the largest and often highly decorated.

Below: Elaborately decorated stones at the back of the recess in the largest cairn at Loughcrew, aligned to receive the equinox sun.

11

GREATER POWERS
Gods and Goddesses

We only see Ireland's deities now through the distorting lenses of later traditions but the Daghdha, the Celtic *dago-Dewios*, is the Indo-European sky deity who became *Deus* in Latin and *Zeus* in Greek. The Celts gave his name to an earlier Irish sun god who built Brú na Bóinne and whose cauldron satisfied everyone, while Lugh, the Celtic god of arts and agriculture, gave Ireland the Lughnasa harvest cult.

Of goddesses, apart from Cailleach Bhéarra and Bóinn there was Meadhbh, donor of Tara's sovereignty, who married and inebriated new kings and took lovers. Bríghid, goddess of poetry and fertility, arrived with the Celtic Brigantes. Her feast at the onset of February, *Oímelg*, 'lactation', the first day of Spring, became St Bridget's, as did her wells, while Macha, Ulster's land goddess's name, originally simply a word for an area of ground, became sacred through Emhain Macha, Navan, and Ard Macha, Armagh.

In this mythologically saturated landscape otherworld beings are associated with every significant feature. Many hills or tumuli contain a *sídh* or a *brú*, otherworld homes of supernatural beings, and quite probably the megalithic carvings relate somehow to lost Stone Age beliefs or myths. Amongst the enigmatic shapes and patterns there are some apparently astronomically inspired, as well as some suggestively female forms at Loughcrew and Sess Kilgreen, and male ones at Dowth and Seefin.

Above: Brú na Bóinne, New Grange, in its unexcavated state.

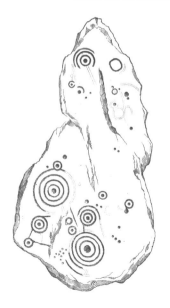

*Above, left and below: Decorated stones from
Knowth and Brú na Bóinne.*

INNER DIVIDES
the fifths of Ireland

The Fír Bolg brothers' division of Ireland into five created a middle section, Mídh (now Westmeath and Meath), centring on Uisneach hill. Huge Beltaine fires welcomed in summer, its well, the Navel of Ireland, fed twelve rivers, Stonehenge stood here before Merlin removed it, and goddess Ériu dwelt here, as did one of the five sacred tribal trees.

Tara, Mídh's royal site, houses two gods: Lugh, foreteller of kings, and intoxicating Maedhbh who slept with them and gave sovereignty; the new kings then drove chariots harnessed to unbroken horses against the stone penis Lia Fáil to make it screech against the axles.

On Ulster's royal hill, Emhain Macha, a sequence of imposing Iron Age round houses stood for centuries, with a Barbary ape's skull buried under one of them. Then a vast circular wooden structure was erected, filled with stones taken from megalithic cairns, burned and buried, making a ritual centre by methods similar to those used at henges two thousand years earlier.

Crúachan, Connacht's hill, has a divinity called Crochain Croidhearg, the Blood-Red of sunset, death and gestation, and the great bulls of Ulster and Connacht fought here, as they did indeed elsewhere.

Leinster's hill, Dún Áilinne, had a large circular structure on it with similarities to Emhain Macha's and its first king's parents were the goddess Bóinn and the rays of the sun.

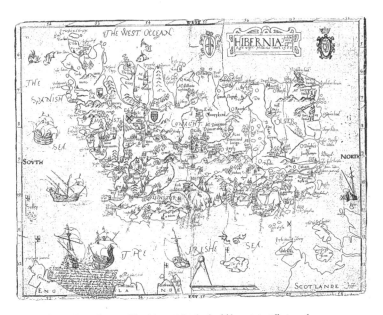

Above: On early maps like this one Meath, the fifth part, is still given the same significance as the other provinces. Below: The Forradh, or Royal Seat, Tara.

THE COUNTRY'S FAIRS
fractals of five

As well as the sacred assembly hills of Ireland's fifths the country's many kingdoms all had their own. Most had mythological significance. The Rock of Cashel, seat of Munster's kings and bishops from the fifth century, belonged to the sovereignty goddess Mór Mumhann, and tales were told of Oisín's struggles here with an Otherworld bull. Clogher had one of Ireland's three great oracle stones, on which gold and silver melded into the stone, and Armagh was symbolically gifted by Dáire, a tribal version of the Daghdha, to Patrick. Pre-Christian effigies survive there, probably of Nuadha of the Tuatha Dé Danann with his silver arm and Labhraidh Loingseach with his asses' ears.

The most important of several assembly places near Tara was Teltown. Annual fairs, presided over by the High Kings, were celebrated with races, wrestling, charioteering, and aquatic fights. Connacht's three Iron Age assembly places, just like Tara, had penis-shaped monoliths, including the elaborately carved Turoe Stone. Ancient Ireland's tribal social structure depended upon these assemblies, and some still survive, including the Lammas Fair at Ballycastle, Antrim, which long ago moved down from its old assembly hill, or Killorglin's Puck Fair in Kerry, while the belief that hills contain otherworld beings extended down to raths, the forts of an early ruling class, whose spirit guardians turn malevolent if disturbed.

Above: An Irish Fairday, Tully, Co. Fermanagh

Up North
Ulster's Mountains

Many Gods live in Ulster's hills. Slieve Donard houses the last pagan king's son, its megalithic tomb being a portal to his domain, while Slieve Gullion's chambered cairn is the triple goddess Cailleach Bhéarra's. She guards land and its sovereignty, receives the last harvest sheaf, and once enticed Fionn Mac Cumhaill inside, to emerge aged and spent.

Knockmany near Clogher is the Daghdha's, its decorated passage cairn aligned both to the noonday sun and Loughcrew, as is Slieve Gullion's. Fionn mac Cumhail's mother lived here while he built the Giant's Causeway, and the Daghdha also has a hill fort near Derry, the Grianan of Aileach. Slieve Beagh's passage cairn, Tyrone, is the tomb of Bith, Noah's son and even Patrick's Slemish has pagan neighbours: a standing stone on a mountain cairn, and what was probably a ritual royal site on Skerry Hill.

A few cult objects have been found on these heights. The Topped Mountain's cairn, Fermanagh, yielded a bronze dagger with a gold pommel, Corleck Hill, Cavan, a stone head with three faces, and from nearby Taghart Hill comes the Ralaghan wooden figure, with quartz fragments in the hole for its phallus. There was a week-long fair held here for Lughnasa, which was commemorated on virtually every height from Belmore in Fermanagh, to Errigal, Donegal, to County Down's Mourne Mountains.

Opposite above: Glenarrif, Co. Antrim.
Below: Giant's Causeway, Co. Antrim built by Fionn Mac Cumhaill.

DOWN SOUTH
the mountains of Munster

Limerick has three fairy mountains, inside which are sídh, otherworld palaces. Cnoc Áine's goddess lives in its hilltop cairn, which at certain times opens to let out the fairies, the Sí, while tribal ancestors inhabit three barrows. At midsummer locals circled them holding burning brands which they then took back to empower their fields. Cnoc Fírinne, the Hill of Truth, houses the king of the Sí, a god of death and fertility who controls the clouds. New stones had to be added to its cairn by pilgrims, and young girls left gifts on the hillside at Bealtaine and Samhain, as well as flowers on its summit at Lughnasa. In the third of these hills, Cnoc Gráinne, lives the sun goddess.

Precious ores have great powers, so Lughnasa was celebrated on the Silvermines hills, whose central peak is Mathair Sliabh, the Mother Mountain. The breasts of the goddess Áine form the Paps of Anu in Cork. On Slieve Mish in Kerry Míl's sons confronted the Tuatha Dé Dannan's queen Banbha and buried their ancestress Scota, while at Slievenamon, Tipperary, Oisín was born. Bodhbh Dearg, king of the Tuatha Dé Dannan, also lives there, in a cairn along with the female Sí, and Kerry's Mount Brandon is also male. It was the sun god's long before St Brendan came.

Opposite above: Upper lake, Killarney.
Below: Gap of Dunlaoe, Kerry.

Out West
the mountains of Connacht

Most famously, Ireland's national saint defeated his worst supernatural opponents on Croagh Patrick, and a great mountain pilgrimage still takes place here on the Sunday nearest to Lughnasa, at the end of July. Hundreds climb up, praying at its shrines, and as much of Ireland's prehistoric gold was mined nearby there are ancient reasons for this veneration.

On Mám Éan, Galway, Lughnasa rituals long stayed alive. On what was called Crom Dubh's Sunday people climbed up to thank the Dark Bent God for the harvest and ask for the earth's continuing fertility. There was much music and dancing, and men from different sides of the mountain fought each other with shillelaghs.

These mountain traditions mostly have little Christian veneer. Knocknashee, Sligo, with its huge hill fort, is the Hill of the Fairies, and Maedhbh, the intoxicating goddess, lives in one of four cairns on Knockmaa, Galway. Finnbheara, the fairies' leader, entices humans into his domain in another of these cairns and Noah's granddaughter, Cesair, is in a third, while on Knocknarea, overlooking Sligo Bay, is Maedhbh's greatest cairn, made from over 40,000 tons of stones. She stands inside this hill spear in hand with her best men, waiting for the right moment to attack Ulster. The father-sun god, the Daghdha, is nearby, in a megalithic complex on Cairn Hill.

Opposite above: Eagle Mountain, Connemara
Below: Head of the Killeries, Connemara.

FACING EAST
mountains of Leinster

Leinster lore is often frustratingly uncertain. Dunamase Rock in Laois, for instance, may once have been so important that Ptolemy put it on his map, but today only a vague tale survives about a treasure inside it guarded by a hound who spews out flames. Equally unclear is the location of Da Dearga, the Red God of Death's house in which Conaire met his end; it was perhaps somewhere in the Dublin Hills.

However the Wicklow hill-tops have many passage cairns, including an enormous one on Baltinglass, with a fine stone basin. Here, as on Seefin and the Sugarloaf, the passages point north, possibly to stellar positions and Brú na Bóinne, which got its quartz from these hills. Kildare's Hill of Allen, however, has well preserved traditions of Fionn mac Cumhaill, and at Ardagh Hill in Longford Midir, king of the Tuatha Dé Dannan, struggled for eons with Eochad Aiream of the Milesians over the fairy maiden Étain. Locals said a giant in the hill pulled children inside, to where passages lead down to his subterranean castle.

The best accounts of Leinster Lughnasa festivities are about Caher Roe's Den on the Backstairs Mountains in Wexford, where, after dining on the year's first potatoes, the locals climbed up for a day of singing, dancing, berry picking and fighting.

Opposite above: Enniskerry, Wicklow.
Below:Dunamase Rock, Co. Laois.

ON THE FRINGES
promontories and coastline

The edges of Ireland were venerated as points of contact with the beyond, and places where early incomers had either landed or were exiled. Uniquely amongst them the Hill of Howth, Dublin, is a shrine to love: here Éadar died from love for goddess Áine and the mountain was the lovers' refuge both of Diarmaid and Gráinne, and Deirdre and the sons of Uislu. By contrast Kerry's promontories hold fierce beings. Balar the thunder god is in Mizen Head, the hag goddess Cailleach Bhéarra in the Beara peninsula and Donn, god of the dead, on an island in Kenmare Bay. Kerry also has the ancestor-mother Scota lying in Slieve Mish, and the Daghdha was on Mount Brandon long before St Brendan. Indeed the myths made him the saint's grandfather.

The Tuatha Dé Dannan are also sacred to the South West, while the brutal Fomhóire ended up north, on Tory island. They created the Giant's Causeway in Antrim long before Fionn Mac Cumhaill, and nearby Fair Head is home to the Grey Man, the sea god Manannán. The Children of Lír, turned into swans, flew for centuries off these headlands before being banished to the wild Atlantic coast for several more hundred years, flying above the final strongholds of the Fír Bolg before they became gods of the Underworld.

Opposite above: Fair Head, Co. Antrim, home to the Grey Man.
Below: Natural Bridges near Kilkee, Co. Clare.

WATERY WAYS
rivers and lakes

Irish waters tell many mythological tales. Lough Owel, Westmeath, was hauled from place to place by giantesses, and in Lough Derg St Patrick met the serpent Corra, the warrior aspect of a triple goddess, who swallowed him. Lough Lagan, Roscommon, also contains a serpent, at Lough na Súil in Sligo Lugh put out Balor's eye, and goddess Áine lives in Lough Gur, Limerick, as a mermaid. Lír's children became swans at Lough Derravarragh, Westmeath, and Eochaidh's great steed's urine (Eochaidh is an epithet of the Daghdha) formed Lough Neagh.

The Boyne celebrates the goddess Bóinn, whose name ultimately derives from the Celtic word for wisdom, as indeed does the mythical Fionn's. He too features in the river's tales. A sacred hazel tree growing beside the Boyne's source dropped the goddess's berries of wisdom into the river, and these were devoured by the salmon which Fionn then ate, giving him his seer's powers.

The Shannon also bears the name of a mother-goddess who gave both fertility and wisdom, and many water rites were performed at Lughnasa. 'Their horses swim in some lakes on Garlic Sunday ... believing this will render them healthy during the rest of the year' an observer wrote in 1682, and 'they ... drive their cattle into some pool or river and therein swim with them.'

Opposite above: Fionnloch, Co. Mayo, in which lurked a great serpent.
Below: Near Derrycunihy Cascade, Killarney.

SPINNING ROUND
circles

Near the end of the Neolithic period which produced the great megalithic monuments henges appeared, large banked and usually ditched circular enclosures with astronomical alignments, which were also often related to elaborate wooden structures. Limerick has the fine Lios, while the largest, the Giant's Ring, is on high ground south of Belfast and Dowth hill has yet another. Some only appear now as crop marks, like Ballybattin near Tara, which was as complex a site as Stonehenge before its 18th century destruction.

Stone circles were constructed in large numbers during the Bronze Age, and appear to have been largely built or inspired by incomers. Ballynoe, near Dundrum in Down, for example, closely resembles circles just across the sea in Cumbria, and the south Munster group are similar to those constructed somewhat earlier in northeast Scotland. Most point in the general direction of important sunsets; Drombeg, Cork, looks towards midwinter's, and Bohonagh circle to equinox sundowns.

Folktales abound: at Clonakilty a quarzite pillar is called the Sun Stone, the stones at Lissyviggeen, Kerry, and the Piper's Stones, Wicklow, are petrified dancers; at Killycluggin, Cavan, they are Crom Dubh's court, at Beaghmore, Tyrone, the 'Dragon's Teeth' and a giant hound, the Callan Mór, was killed beside the Ballybriest circles, Derry, some of the many in Ulster constructed on the Sperrin mountains.

Above: Ballymore, near Dundrum, Co. Down, a large diameter ring (over 100ft) of close-set irregular stones with double portals facing downhill, very similar to circles on the Cumbrian coast. Below: The circles of south-west Ireland have recumbent stones and many cup marks, and use stones rich in quartz, very like circles in north-east Scotland; left: A partly ruined circle in Co. Kerry; right: Stone Circle at Slieve na Greidle, Co. Down.

STANDING ALONE
monoliths

The ancient standing stones that are found throughout Ireland vary from the stumpy to tall elegant ones like the 21 ft Dunfeeny stone in Mayo. A medieval poem 'The Stones of Ireland' claims they mark heroes' graves, and some, as at Punchestown and Longstone, Kildare, or Dumnahare and Carrownacaw, Down, do stand over Bronze Age burials.

Others may be astronomically oriented and some intriguing traditions exist. The Stone of the Tree, in county Limerick, is part of a supernatural tree in a nearby lough, the mortally wounded Cuchulainn tied himself to a stone bearing his name in Louth so as to fight on, and holed stones used in fertility rites include the Aghade stone, Carlow, through which new babies were passed, and the Hole Stone of Doagh, Antrim, where couples pledged their troth.

The Iron Age produced carved and shaped monoliths, like the Turoe and Castlestrange stones and the Lia Fáil. All of these obviously phallic objects stood in tribal assembly places. Later, ogham inscriptions commemorating individuals were incised on monoliths, including the 17 ft high Faunkill stone, Cork. Christianity also accepted stone magic, by putting new imagery on monoliths, creating high crosses, and sanctifying some stones' powers to give cures, float, fly, bear the shapes of saints' knees or feet, or protect child-bearing women through carved stone Sheela-na-Gigs. Nor should we forget the Blarney Stone's magic powers over speech.

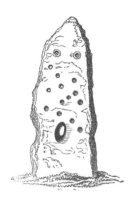

Above: These stones illustrate their magical uses. Oaths and wishes were made binding in the top left stone, the virility of kings by the Lia Fáil or Pillar Stone at Tara (top middle), and great men were honoured with ogham inscriptions on standing stones such as this one (right) at Monataggart, Co. Cork.

Below: Women touched stone Sheela na Gigs such as this one at Taughboy Church, Co. Roscommon, to receive their protection. Below: Babies were reborn through holes in other stones. Below Right: Ogham Stones near Durrus.

Vanishing Points
meeting places

This sacred landscape included many magical trees. Some were immortal totems and five represented Ireland's fifths, including one at Uisneach that fell when St Patrick arrived. Later, St Kevin had a miraculous yew and willow, and St Columcille an oak. Holy wells often have trees near them to which rags are tied, as at Fore in Westmeath, St Olcan's at Cranfield, Antrim or St Flannan's, Clare, and all thorn trees belong to the fairies, who bring misfortune to anyone cutting them.

As earlier peoples, spirits and gods live underneath this landscape there are entrances through which they can come to us from the beyond or which allow us, sometimes, to visit them. Inevitably therefore there are taboos against damaging these portals, in particular against interfering with raths, trees, standing stones or tumuli.

Subterranean places are particularly potent, projecting as they do into the mystical underworld, so Irish miners refused to be below ground at midnight, in case they were spirited away. Keshcorran cave on Carrowkeel hill, Sligo, is an important spirit entrance, and the home of the goddess Morrigan, while The Three Caves of Ireland, at Oweynagat at Crúachain, in Roscommon, Howth, near Dublin, and Dunmore, Kilkenny, are equally significant. In Oweynagat cave people disappear into other realms and spirits come through into this one at Samhain, disguised as cats.

Left: Sacred trees had powerful roots penetrating to the underworld, as with this one at St. Patrick's Well, Armagh, while birds had the magical property to fly into and from the beyond, or nest in caves on the rocky membrane between the here and now and the other side.

Below: Dunkerry Cave, Co. Antrim, an atmospheric meeting place of the elements any time of the year.

New Heights
Christian complexes

Christianity was well established by AD 431, when the pope sent Bishop Palladius to the Irish. The first churches were often placed on hills near royal ones that had been pagan ritual sites, such as Dunshaughlin near Tara, or Armagh, and old powers got new meanings.

Patrick's pascal flame quickly outshone Tara's pagan fires, holy wells and venerated hills were given Christian dedications, and even sacred trees were kept, as at Derry or at Ross in Carlow. Ironically, Patrick's 'God-sent' visions, and indeed, the physical and mental conditions that caused them, bear remarkable parallels with the shamans' trance-induced hallucinations which inspired Irish megalithic imagery, though Patrick would never have accepted this.

Quite commonly the old sacred places found a new religious identity: Clogher of the gold oracle stone had been a ritual royal site long before becoming a bishop's seat and Ardagh's cathedral stands on a hill that contains the sídh of a Tuatha Dé Danann otherworld king.

At Skerry, Antrim, a church was built on the ashes of Patrick's slave master's house, in a process much like the creation of Emhain Macha's ritual site, and Saint Bridget, or Brighid, acquired many of her namesake's places and festivals, including an enormous oak at Kildare, and the fire festival of Oímelg at the beginning of February, marking the beginning of Spring.

Above: The church on St. MacDara's Island, Galway, and St. Columba's Oratory, Ceanannus Mór, Meath (Kells), are typical Irish Early Christian, small shrine-like, sacred places, very different in scale and feeling to grandiose later buildings like Cashel cathedral (below), in Tipperary's Golden Vale.

TURNING STONES
cursing and curing

Bulláns are often found at old church sites and holy wells. These are
flat stones with round indentations in which sit water worn stones
or pebbles, which were often said to grow in the holy wells and are
frequently called cursing stones. At Kilmoon, Clare, a victim's mouth
would be twisted awry by the stones being turned while reciting the
individual's name, two stones in the Joyce country, Connemara, brought
evil on a false accuser if the slandered person turned the stones and
called down harm, and on Iniskea island off Achill, anyone seeking
revenge turned a *bullán* stone by a well three times while praying that
their enemy would 'not prosper or get the length of life'.

They also brought cures, if turned *'déiseal'*, or sun-wise. A healing
stone at St Conall's well, Donegal cured most ills, as did the thirteen
stones of Toberaraght well and the seventeen stones at Toomour
altar, both in Sligo. Another Sligo *bullán*, at Killery, was famous
for its curing powers, and water collected from the *bulláns* cured
ailments too. Turning stones to call up supernatural powers must
be extremely ancient. New Grange has circular depressions in one
stone basin, and many more elsewhere. They are common to many
sites and integral to the free-standing neolithic 'cup and ring' rock
carvings of Staigue Bridge and Derrynablaha, Kerry.

Opposite left: St. Bridget's Stone, Killinagh, nr Blacklion. Opposite right: Altar at Toomour, with Dumb-bell Stone, and "dicket stones".

This page, top: The Little Altar, with Stones, Island of Inishmurray. Left: Clocha Breacha Altar with cursing stones, Island of Inishmurray. Below: Altar at Toberaraght.

The intense belief in the bulláns' powers led to their inclusion in popular Christianised beliefs. Similar sites are found all over Ireland.

WELLS
springing up within

Countless wells were blessed by Patrick, including Altadaven, Tyrone, Struel Wells, Down, St Patrick's, Sligo and Tobar Phádraig, Galway, while at Eithne's Well, Donegal, supplicants walk round ancient cairns and standing stones before washing their feet. Similar rites occur at many others, each a cure to particular troubles, from jealousy to arthritis, and weak eyes to tooth ache. Gleann na nGealt's well in Kerry cures insanity, thanks to its water's high levels of lithium, even calming the 'Mad Sweeney', and swallowing one of Cranfield, (Antrim)'s amber pebbles prevented drowning on the voyage to America.

As many of Saint Brighid's wells first belonged to the fertility goddess they are visited by women wanting babies or safe deliveries. Her well at Faughart, Louth, was beside her father's farm, where she produced vast quantities of food, while one at Liscannor, Clare, aids conception, as does Brideswell, Westmeath, over which an Irish earl built a chapel as a thankyou for his many children.

Opposite left: St. Declan's Well, Ardmore in 1830. Opposite right: St. Molaise's Well, Island of Inishmurray.

This page, left: Well and Altars at Tubbernalt, nr Sligo. Below: St. Senan's Well, County Clare.

Many holy wells have trees growing beside them, to which supplicants tie pieces of clothing or messages. Often they are dedicated to local saints who are unknown outside their home territories, like St. Moling of Carlow or St. Mogue in Leitrim. Often too fishes live in the wells, and keep their water pure.

OVER THE WATER
island ways to the beyond

Ireland's subsiduary islands were repositories of ancient powers. Tory, Donegal, was the ferocious Fomhóire's citadel, the Aran Islands harboured the Fír Bolg and Donn, god of the dead, lived on another off Kerry. Boa island, Lough Erne, named after the warrior goddess Badhbh, has a remarkable Janus-headed Iron Age statue, and the islands to the west were near entrances to the Otherworld or to Tír na nÓg, the Land of the Young.

Early Christian communities also favoured islands, as they offered some serenity and natural protection, as well as ease of communication by boat. Nendrum in Strangford Lough, the earliest island monastery, was followed by Devenish in Lough Erne, Lambay off Dublin, and others on the Arran Islands, Tory, Holy Island, Clare, the Blaskets, Kerry, and Caher Island, Mayo.

The monks particularly liked uninhabited islands as evil powers cannot cross water, and therefore unpolluted communities could flourish on them. An extreme example of this is Skellig Michael off Kerry, a rock rising out of the Atlantic which Irish monks lived on for five hundred years. Indeed the search for 'clean' islands led them far away, as St Brendan's tales suggest. In their frail leather-covered curraghs Irish monks discovered and settled on Iceland before the Vikings. When they appeared the monks fled, rowing off westwards, to an unknown fate.

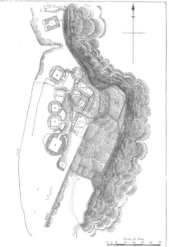

*Above and left: The Atlantic island
monastery of Skellig Michael, 8 miles
off the Kerry coast. For centuries
multitudes of pilgrims performed
death-defying penances on it and
kissed the cross engraved on the end
of a narrow stone projecting out over
the sea from its highest point. The
island was the last in a chain of
prominent features dedicated at a
very early date to the dragon-slaying
archangel St. Michael, patron saint of
warriors and mariners. across Europe.
Others include St. Michael's Mount
in Cornwall, Mont Saint Michel in
France and Monte Gargano on the
Adriatic coast of Italy.*

43

GAZETEER OF MOUNTAINS

ALTADAVIN, Alt a' Deamhain, Tyrone, on Blaeberry Sunday, in late July, the Lughnasa customs were to climb the hill, pick berries, have sports and dancing and sit in St Patrick's Chair. He had preached from it, and confined a serpent in a nearby rock.

AN DÚNA, Portacloy, Mayo, a promontory fort. The local youth ate the first potatoes before gathering here for Lughnasa customs and dancing on the last Sunday of July.

ANASCAUL, Abhainn an Scáil, Kerry. Cú Chulainn fought a giant here for a week. Three cairns bear his name; Lughnasa customs were held on 'Cucuhulain's House', 1814 ft.

ARDAGH HILL, Ardachadh, Longford, or Brí Léith, the sídh of Mídir, king of the Tuatha Dé Danann. He brought Étaín Echraidhe, an Ulster princes, here. She was turned into a pool by his wife, became a dragon fly and flew to Aonghus at Brú na Bóinne. On the first August Sunday bilberries are picked, though a giant in the hill drags pickers into his lair.

AUGHRIS HEAD, Sligo, on Garland Sunday, at Lughnasa, after eating the first potatoes rounds were made of a holy well, berries eaten, games played and much match making done. Lights appear in the fairy fort, when the 'Good People' dance.

BLACKSTAIRS MOUNTAINS, Wexford, Caher Roe's Den, is a cave of Crom Cruach. He once lured a girl in, wanting to drag her below, but locals stopped her. A popular Lughnasa festival held on the last July Sunday.

BALLYHEADY HILL, Cavan. On it is a megalithic cairn with a Bronze Age burial cist. Lughnasa customs observed here up to the early 1900s

BELLALEENAN HILL, Cavan. After St Patrick defeated Crom Cruach on Slieveanieran he blessed the well here; at Lughnasa there was dancing, singing and sports and visits to the well. A fairy road is nearby.

BELMORE MOUNTAIN, Fermanagh. A cairn on its summit contains a passage and cruciform chamber. Lughnasa customs, sports and a fair continued into the 1950s

BEN SCARDAUN, Leitrim, on Garland Sunday, the last in July, the locals ate the first potatoes, met by two standing stones at a lake, played music, and climbed up to strew flowers and collect bilberries.

CAIRNS HILL, Sligo, the Daghdha's resting place. On its summit is Meadhbh's vast cairn, calculated to contain over 40,000 tons of stones, covering a megalithic passage and its chambers. This goddess lives in it, waiting for the right moment to attack Ulster.

CARNTOGHER HILL, Carnán Tachair, Derry, its hill-top cairn is inhabited by a giant, Tachar Mór, below it is a stone circle and a monolith. Fionn's hound Bran made the lake, and groups climbed up on Bilberry Sunday to for Lughnasa celebrations.

CARN TREUNA HILL, Donegal. On Bilberry Sunday, at the beginning of August, the young went up the hill, made bilberry bracelets for the girls, told stories, sang, danced, and finally left the bracelets on the hill.

CARRICKATUKE MOUNTAIN, Armagh, on the summit was a cairn, but now only St Patrick's chair remains. He tamed a ferocious bull here. Lughnasa customs on Blaeberry Sunday. 'Not long ago thousands would come.'

CARRICKBYRNE HILL, Wexford is topped by a cairn, used in the Lughnasa festival held on the second July Sunday. There is a hidden magical cave inside it.

CHURCH MOUNTAIN, Sliabh Gad, Wicklow, the mountain was climbed for Lughnasa harvest rites, berry picking and games. There is a chambered cairn on the peak, and a holy well with medical powers.

CORLECK HILL, Cavan, a prehistoric stone head with three faces was found on this Lughnasa site.

Glen of the Downs, Wicklow.

There is also had a holy well.

CROAGH PATRICK, Mayo, 2,510ft, the peak on which St Patrick prayed and fasted for forty days, asking for God's favours and constantly surrounded by demonic birds, which he defeated with St Brigid's bell. He also defeated the old god Lugh here, though the main pilgrimage day is still at Lughnasa time.

CROAGHAUN, Achill, Mayo, 2,192 ft, young people eat the first potatoes and climb this 2,139 ft hill on Garlic Sunday at the end of July, and pick berries

DOWNPATRICK HEAD, Mayo, on Garland Sunday, the locals ate the first potatoes before coming here for Lughnasa customs of singing, dancing, sports and faction fighting. The pilgrims passed a great chasm, then went to an ancient church and finally the cliff edge.

DRUNG HILL, Kerry, is topped by a megalithic cairn; on Pilgrimage Sunday each house came with a cake and food, cooked on the summit, strew flowers and held a cattle fair.

DUBLIN HILLS, probable site of Da Dearga's Hostel, where king Conaire was killed

GAINMHE HILL, Donegal, the highest on Rosguill peninsula. The young gathered here, on a late summer Sunday, told stories, sang, and buried the flowers they had brought. There was a dancing competition, and the winner chose any girl he liked for his wife.

HILL OF ALLEN, Cnoc Almhaine, Kildare, associated with stories of Fionn mac Cumhaill.

HILL OF HOWTH, Beann Éadar, Dublin. Éadar, a warrior died here for love of Áine, the land goddess of Munster whose sídh was in Cnoc Áine, Limerick. Diarmaid and Gráinne and also Deirdre and the three sons of Uislu all took refuge here.

KESHCORRAN, Céis Chorainn, Sligo, has a cairn on its peak. It was given to Corann the harper by the Tuatha Dé Danann, and an enchanted sow was killed here. Garland Sunday observed by large crowds gathering near some caves used since neolithic times.

KINAWLEY, Cill Náile, Fermanagh. On 'Donagh Sunday' at the end of July the Lughnasa festivities included gathering round a great rock, and a visit to St Náile's holy well.

KNOCKAINY, Cnoc Áine, Limerick, sacred hill of goddess Áine. A cairn covers her sídh. One of Munster's three fairy hills, the locals climbed it holding flaming torches on midsummer's eve, and the goddess sometimes appeared in human form.

KNOCKFEERINA, Cnoc Fírinne, Limerick, 'the hill of truth', one of the three fairy hills of Munster. Donn Fírinne, god of death and fertility, is now a Fairy King living inside it. He collects the clouds. Stones were added to his cairn at the start of Lughnasa celebrations.

KNOCKGREAN, Cnoc Gráinne, Limerick, the home of Gráinne the sun goddess and one of the three fairy hills of Munster. Its peak is Knockseefinn, the hill of Fionn's fairy mound.

KNOCKMAA, Galway. On top is the massive neolithic cairn of goddess Meadhbh, of inebriation, sovereignty and horses, who takes many lovers and makes the land fertile.

KNOCKMANY, Cnoc Meánach, Clogher, its summit

Gougane Barra, Cork.

Dunamase, Co. Laois.

cairn has a megalithic chamber, the home of Fionn Mac Cumhaill; many incised stones and alignments to the noonday sun and Loughcrew

KNOCKNADOBAR, Cnoc na dTobar, Kerry, 2,207 ft, Lughnasa celebrations on the summit near six standing stones on the last July Sunday. St Fursa's well here was also visited.

KNOCKNASHEE, Cnoc na Sí, Sligo, the 'Hill of the Fairies,' a huge limestone plateau topped by a large hill fort and two cairns.

KNOCKNAREA, Cnoc na Ría, Sligo. On its summit, 1,078 ft, is Meadhbh's enormous cairn, inside which she stands in a chamber, holding her spear and with her best fighting men.

KNOCKSHEGOWNa, Cnoc Sídh Úna, Tipperary, a place of fairy revels and magic, where the Lughnasa customs and games were on Garland Sunday in mid July.

LEAFRIN HILL, Donegal, an ancient fort, with a souterrain. The young gathered to pick blaeberries and drank broth made from a long grass.

LOUGHCREW, Sliabh na Caillí, Meath The largest of this important hill ridge's thirty passage cairns has a highly decorated stone in its chamber which is bathed by the equinoctial sun. Intriguingly the harvest goddess Cailleach Bhéarra's cairn on Slieve Gullion is oriented towards Loughcrew, the other hill to bear her name.

LOUGHSALT MOUNTAIN, Cnoc a' Liathain, Donegal; the 'Blaeberry Sundays' brought crowds of young here for dancing, singing, games, match making and bilberry picking.

MOUNTAINS (CONTINUED)

Ballina, Co. Mayo.

MAGHERINTEMPLE, Cavan, on the first Sunday of August people came to the ruins of 'St Patrick's temple'. A grease issuing from a stone cured any disease, and the saint had resuscitated a bull here.

MÁM ÉAN, Galway, a high pass in the Maamturk mountains where St Patrick blessed Connemara. Its Lughnasa assembly honoured St Patrick's defeat of Crom Dubh, probably this replaced an older mythological struggle between the gods Balar and Lugh

MOUNT BRANDON, Cnoc Bréanainn, Kerry, the beehive hut on its peak was the dwelling of St Brendan, before he left on his voyages in 'a wicker boat covered with ox skins'.

MULLINAKILL, Kilkenny. This is the birthplace of St Moling, who has a cave and a well here. The hill was a Lughnasa assembly place.

MULLYASH HILL, Monaghan, still attracted large crowds for Blaeberry Sunday in 1942. There were sports, dancing and competitions and visits to a stone with a giant's footprint.

PAPS OF ANU, the breasts of the goddess Ana or Dana, Cork. Lughnasa customs took place here, with berry picking, games and competitions.

ROCK OF BARNANE, Tipperary. On Rock Sunday at the end of July the people climb the 1,577 ft high hill, for Lughnasa customs and games.

SEEFIN, Suídhe Fionn, Cork. Lughnasa rites were held after visits to its summit cairn.

SHEEHAUN HILL, Leitrim, Lughnasa customs observed here in July and August.

SILVERMINES HILLS, Limerick, in their heart is a small peak called Máthair Sliabh; stones were added to its cairn as part of the Lughnasa customs, Silver, lead and zinc were mined here since prehistoric times.

SKERRY HILL, Antrim, St Patrick's slave master's fort was here. On Patrick's return he immolated himself rather than submit to Christianity and a church was built on it.

SKELP HILL, Tyrone, in late summer bilberry picking and games were performed here, including attempts to lift a large stone.

SKELP, Sceilp a' Mhadaidh, Mayo. People ate the first potatoes and gathered on the last July Sunday, Garlic Sunday, beside a ruin for Lughnasa customs and games. A girl was chosen to make bilberry pies.

SLEMISH, Antrim, the mountain on which St Patrick looked after flocks as a slave.

SLIEVE BLOOM between Leix and Offaly, where Fionn lived in hiding as a child. Lughnasa customs and games were held on this 1,734 ft peak on the last Sunday of July.

SLIEVE CALLAN, Sliabh Colláinn, Clare, a 1,200 ft mountain with several megalithic monuments on it. The Lughnasa gathering here was on Crom Dubh's Sunday in early August. Flowers were strewn, and there were games and dancing.

SLIEVE DONARD, Sliabh Donairt, Mourne Mountains, Down. Parthalán, father of one of the earliest races, buried his son in its megalithic cairn. Later it became the entrance to the underworld realm of Donairt, one of Patrick's mountain guardians, set to watch over Ireland until the Last Judgement

Doonass Falls, Castleconnell, Limerick.

49

Mountains (continued)

SLIEVE GULLION, Sliabh gCuilinn, the highest mountain in Armagh. The passage cairn on it is Cailleach Bhéarra's, and is also oriented to Sliabh na Caillí, Loughcrew. Her sheaf from the harvest was hung over the table at harvest supper. Lughnasa customs observed here well into the 20th century.

SLIABH AN IARANN, the Iron Mountain, Sligo. The Tuatha Dé Danann first landed here from a mystic cloud here. Lughnasa rites were held at Pulty, a hole which a stream falls into, at Bellavally Gap's two fairy cairns, and on the summit, 'to salute the summer'.

SLIEVE BEAGH, Clogher, in the passage cairn on its peak is Bith, Noah's grandson, on one slope is St Patrick's Chair, a chair-shaped stone which he christianised, and a holy well.

SLIEVE CROOB, Down, Lughnasa customs were performed around its megalithic cairn. Stones were added to the cairn, music and sports played.

SLIEVE MISH, Sliabh Mís, Kerry, a mountain range near Tralee. The sons of Míl landed nearby, at Beltaine, and met Banbha of the Tuatha Dé Danann and her druids here.

SLIEVENAMON, Sliabh na mBan, Tipperary. Fionn pursued an otherworld woman into this hill but she slammed the door on his thumb, since when he sees the future by sucking it.

SLIEVE RUSHEN, Cavan. In a cave, Tory Hole, on its west side Lughnasa rites observed on Tory Hole Sunday in early August. A fiddler once disappeared inside it, but his music and fairy dancing are still heard.

Ballynahinch, Co. Mayo.

SLIEVE SNAGHT, Sliabh Sneachta, the highest in Inishowen, with a well for eye troubles called Tobar na Súl. On the last July Sunday the young assembled here for heatherberry picking, dances and games, near where St Patrick destroyed a great serpent.

TAGHART HILL, Cavan, the week-long Lughnasa feast here included dancing, singing and games. A prehistoric wooden figure found at its foot has a hole for its missing phallus with fragments of quartz in it.

TOPPED MOUNTAIN, Fermanagh, has a multiple cist cairn, 90 ft across and 12 ft high. A cist here contained a bronze dagger with a gold pommel, an urn and a cremation. On Bilberry Sunday, the third in July, the locals climbed to pick the berries.

TORY HILL, Kilkenny. On its 966 ft high summit pagan worship happened. Fionn and his hound hunted here, a serpent lives in its lake and its Lughnasa festivities were popular.

TRISTIA, Truiste, Mayo, an all-night vigil was held beside its holy wells, on 'Garland Sunday' in late July. One cured eye troubles, the other jealousy.

TULLAGHAN, Sligo, an Ox Mountain hill with three cashels and a holy well. During Lughnasa festivities 'the itinerant dealers sold out their poteen and gingerbread as fast as they could', fiddlers and pipers played, and there were many games.

WICKLOW MOUNTAINS have many megalithic cairns on their peaks, including Seefin and Croneblane with its chamber's vast stone cap called Fionn Mac Cumhaill's hurling stone. The highest peak is Lugnaquilla, 3,039 ft.

Killiney, Wicklow.

CIRCLES, CAIRNS & MEGALITHIC SITES

Mainly these sites were created circa 2,000 – 3,000 BC, but continued to be ritually important for millennia. Diodorus Siculus wrote about one, in the first century BC:

'there is in this island a magnificent sacred precinct of Apollo and a notable temple that is adorned with many votive offerings and is spherical in shape.'

ATHGREANY, the 'Field of the Sun' Piper's Stones, Wicklow, fourteen boulders in a circle with a possible midsummer sunrise alignment; legend says they were people turned to stone for dancing on a Sunday, and that the fairies play the bagpipes at midnight.

BALLYBATTIN near Tara, until the mid 18th century this astonishing complex with external bank, elaborate stone circles and avenue was largely intact. Now only crop marks remain.

BALLYBRIEST dual court cairn, Derry, on the slopes of Slieve Gallion, built directly on the ashes of a huge fire and earlier ritual deposits; many other megalithic cairns nearby.

BALTINGLASS HILL, Wicklow, on it are the remains of a massive passage cairn, 90 ft across and retained by a double ring of stones. A passage leads to a chamber with a beautifully cut stone basin. The earliest passage cairn points north, a stellar alignment, and has incised diamond patterns as at Fourknocks and Seefin.

BALLYKEEL DOLMEN, Armagh. It has a huge cairn, 90 ft long, with the dolmen made with 7ft high portals and a large cap stone at its south end.

BALLYMACDERMOT, Armagh, a court cairn, 600 ft up the mountain, has three chambers.

BALLYNOE stone circle, about 70 stones, some 7ft high, aligned to the midwinter sunset.

BEAGHMORE, Tyrone, the most important of the many megalithic complexes on the Sperrins, it consists of nine stone circles, and many cairns, portals and avenues. One alignment is to the summer solstice and the complex is dated between 1500 and 800 BC

BELTANY stone circle, Donegal, associated with Beltaine, the beginning of summer, is 145 ft across, with 64 upright stones.

BRÚ NA BÓINNE, Newgrange, Dowth and Knowth. This famous and remarkable site, oriented towards midwinter sunrise, dates back to circa 3,000 BC. Nearby are the equally important sites of Dowth and Knowth.

BOHONAGH circle, Cork, 13 stone circle aligned to equinox sunsets

CARROWKEEL, Sligo, 14 megalithic passage cairns high on the Bricklieve Mountains, built circa 3,000 to 2,000 BC and aligned to various solar and lunar settings. Cairn G has a light box like New Grange, for the summer solstice.

CARROWMORE, Sligo, apparently has the oldest megalithic complex in Ireland, dating back to 5,400 BC. 55 passage cairns have been recorded here, forming a ring round an empty area, with many opening towards a large cairn in the middle which covered seven skeletons and large quantities of charcoal, possibly the site of a ritual fire.

DROMBEG, Cork, 17 stone circle with tall portal stones, opposite a 7 ft long axial stone with two cup marks. In a pit near the centre were the bones of an Iron Age youth and a broken urn. The alignment is to the winter solstice sunset.

FOURKNOCKS, chambered cairn, Meath, a short passage leads to a large chamber with three recesses. Twelve stones have powerful angular patterns and zigzags.

The orientation is to the north, on a stellar or lunar alignment, as at Seefin and Baltinglass.

GIANT'S RING, Belfast. The largest ritual site in Ireland. A circular earth bank, 12 ft high, encloses an area about 600 ft across, containing the remains of a neolithic dolmen. Outside it was an oval enclosure 300 ft long of double rows of huge posts, with a smaller one inside it containing a planked walkway leading to a platform.

GLENISHEEN wedge cairn, Clare consists of two long sidestones supporting a roof slab and in it was found the Glensheen Gold Collar, dated to the Bronze Age.

KILCLOONEY dolmen, Donegal, has 6ft high portals supporting a massive 20 ft cap-stone

KILLYCLUGGIN, Cavan, one of the three elaborately carved Iron Age stones, which stood, decorated with beaten gold beside a stone circle until St Patrick destroyed it, so as to break the pagan god Crom Cruach's power.

KNOCKMANY chambered cairn, Tyrone, magnificent megalithic sandstone slabs carved with great complexity. It is aligned south towards the midday sun and Loughcrew.

LEGANANNY dolmen, perhaps the most graceful one in Ireland, a 10 ft granite slab resting on two slender 6ft pillars and a pointed end stone.

LIOS, Limerick, a circular henge made of standing stones backed by a 3 ft earthen bank. There are Lughnasa and Bealtaine sunrise alignments, and two entrance stones point towards the sunsets of Samhain and Oímelg. Circa 2,000 BC

LISSYVIGGEEN, circle Kerry, 7 uprights surrounded by a circular bank and with two large outliers beyond the bank.

LOUGHCREW, Sliabh na Caillí, Meath, a hill ridge with over 30 chambered cairns on it. 'Cairn T' has

a corbelled chamber and 27 decorated stones, while another has a white pillar stone illuminated by the equinox sun and a third has finely worked spirals as at New Grange.

PIPER'S STONES, Broadleas Commons, Kildare, a circle of almost continuous broad granite boulders, with some quartz.

POULNABRONE dolmen, Clare, stands on a limestone platform, circa 2,500 BC; the defleshed remains of about 20 adults and 6 children were found in it.

PROLEEK dolmen, Louth, a huge cap stone poised on three pointed tall stones

SESS KILGREEN passage cairn, Tyrone, with 11ft long chamber, its endstone decorated with a double concentric ring around another smaller concentric ring, facing the summer solstice. The name incorporates that of Gráinne, the sun goddess.

SEEFIN passage cairn, Wicklow, Blessington Mountain. A passage leads to a chamber with five recesses; two stones at the chamber's entrance have concentric diamond shapes and five lines on an entrance roof stone point north. It is one of only three aligned to the stars, and all use diamond patterns.

SLIEVE GULLION passage cairns, the southern one, 'Cailleach Bhéarra's house', is one of the largest passage cairns in Ulster, over 80 ft in diameter, and dates to about 3,000 BC. Its passage points towards another hill with her name, Sliabh na Caillí, Loughcrew.

TARA, Meath, its passage cairn, Dumha na nGiall, the Mound of the Hostges aligns to sunrise in early February and November, the beginning of Spring and Winter, its backstone's carvings show circles and arcs. Two gold torcs found in it date from about 2,000 BC

TEMPLEBRYAN stone circle, Clonakilty Cork, four of nine visible stones still upright, one made of quartz and called the 'sun stone' locally.

ASSEMBLY PLACES & FAIRS

These assemblies and fairs were essential for the ancient Irish kingdoms, as no towns existed until the Vikings built Ireland's first urban centres at Limerick, Waterford, Wexford, Dublin and Galway. Thus began Ireland's first market towns, which have nobly continued many of the traditions and customs of the ancient fairs to the present day.

ARD MACHA (Armagh); this and Emhain Macha (Navan) were the sacred assembly sites of the Ulaidh. Navan became a ritual site after an enormous round house was filled with boulders, burnt and covered with turves. The importance of the large round houses under it is indicated by the barbary ape's skull found beneath one floor. The Oenach Macha was held nearby.

BALLYCASTLE Lammas Fair, (Antrim), a surviving Lughnasa fair; a promontory fort here is called

Dunaneny, the fort of the oenach. Probably the assembly fair of a local kingdom.

BOYNE River, Meath, early August Lughnasa customs at several locations had horses and cattle made to 'swim across the river as a charm against fairies and certain diseases.'

CARMAN, the unidentified Leinster assembly place. Its week-long oenach had horse races, laments for the dead at royal burial mounds, recitation of lineages, and religious rites. The Leinster king presided, as lesser kings showed off their young men's skills.

CASHEL, Tipperary, capital of the Eóghanacht clan, its name derived from the Latin 'castellum'. This family ruled Munster until Brian Boru took over in the 10th century. Muirhertach O Brien later handed it over to the church and Patrick met Oisín here.

CRÚACHAN (Roscommon), the sacred heart of

54

Grianan of Aileach, Donegal.

Connacht, one of the great royal assembly sites along with Tara, Emhain Macha and Dún Ailinne. Games, judgements, sacred rituals, inauguration of kings and feasting were held here at Lughnasa.

DÚN ÁILINNE, (Kildare), ritual royal site of Leinster associated with Findfile, whose mother was Bóinne and his father the sun's rays. There were remarkable 13 ft high wooden pallisaded structures here; a large oval leading to a circular enclosure.

DUNAMASE ROCK, (Laois), a 150 ft high rock possibly mentioned by Ptolemy. Leinster kings held it until Strongbow got it in his wife's dowry.

KILLORGLIN Puck Fair, Kerry, a surviving Lughnasa fair, held in August and presided over by a large buck goat set on a platform for the fair's duration.

GRIANÁN OF AILEACH, (Donegal) a 17 ft high cashel built by the Daghdha and named after Gráinne the sun goddess. It was an inauguration site for the O'Neills.

LOUGH GUR, Limerick. At its oenach, a mile from Cnoc Áine, 'the horses of the Fiana ran, and the race-loving Munstermen's horses; they held three famous contests on the green of Muiridh's sons.'

LOUGHKEERAN, Loch Ciarán, Mayo, at Garland Sunday's gathering butter was thrown into the lake, cattle halters tied to a tree and horses swum in the lake.

LOUGH NALARSACH, Loch Chill Eascrach, Galway, on Garland Sunday the Lughnasa customs included horse swimming races.

LOUGH OWEL, Westmeath, had a Lughnasa festival on the first August Sunday, with horse swimming races.

TARA, (Meath) Ireland's greatest royal hill. Its earliest structure, the Mound of the Hostages, is from about 3,000 BC; goddess Bóinn is here, and each king married goddess Maedhbh in the Bán Fheis ritual,

which brought salmon to the rivers, good calves to the cows, and much milk and wheat.

TELTOWN, Tailtiu (Meath) Ireland's most famous oenach, assembly fair, was held here, presided over by high-kings, and battles between rivals were frequent. The last high king presided in 1168, but the fair continued into the 18th century. There was horse swimming, wrestling, mock battles and 'Teltown Marriages' when couples married for a year, before deciding whether or not to continue.

UISNEACH (Westmeath), a 600 ft hill. Two huge ritual fires burnt here from Neolithic times. This is Mídh, the centre of Ireland, its well the source of twelve rivers, and Ériu, the country's goddess, lies under the Ail na Mirenn, the Rock of the Portions, from which radiate the divisions of Ireland. According to Giraldus Cambrensis Stonehenge originally stood here.

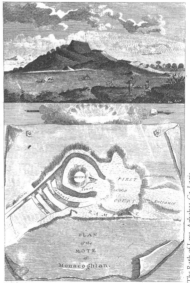

Published by John Jones, N°41 Barrde Street, Dublin.

The Rath of Lara, Aghaboe, Co. Laois.

GLOSSARY OF IRISH NAMES

ÁINE, or Anu, a land-goddess, sometimes a daughter of Manannán, the sea god, or of Eoghabal, king of the otherworld dwelling below Cnoc Áine; ancestress of the Eoghanacht dynasty of Munster, she lives in Lough Gur, Limerick, as a mermaid.

BALAR, the 'flashing one', god of thunder and sky storms. His eye destroys enemies and he lives in Mizen Head; in Britain he lives in Bolerion, Cornwall, and the Hebridees.

BADHBH, warrior goddess and announcer of death, she appears as a scald crow, as these hover over battle fields. A form of the triple-goddess Danu, she is the Banshee, the badhbh caointe. Boa island, Lough Erne, bears her name.

BANBHA, the Tuatha Dé Dannan's queen, brought 150 women and three men to Ireland, 'the island of Banbha of the women'. She survived the Flood by standing on Tul Toinne hill beside the Shannon.

BODHBH DEARG, of the Tuatha Dé Dannan, a warlord deity, 'king of the Otherworld of Munster', his sidh is in Slievenamon, Tipperary, and he is friend of the Daghdha

BÓINN, White Cow goddess, the dispenser of wisdom. The Boyne gives out her wisdom and poetry and the Milky Way flows from her. She mates with the Daghdha, bringing fertility to the world and Fionn, of the wisdom and second sight, was their child.

BRENDAN, an early saint associated with Mount Brandon, Kerry. Legends abound about his extraordinary voyages and he is represented as the grandson of the Daghdha, to whom the mountain was previously dedicated.

BRIGHID, the 'exalted one', goddess of poetry and agricultural fertility, her feast, Oímelg, 'lactation', is the first day of Spring. A triple-formed daughter of the Daghdha is the guardian goddess of domestic animals and an aspect of the mother-goddess.

CAILLEACH BHÉARRA, a manifestation of the land-goddess, she changes from hag to young girl to lure youths into her depths and originates from a belief in a cow-goddess on a western island. Standing stones are often people or animals transformed by her. Her sidh is in Slieve Gullion's passage cairn, she lives in the Beara peninsula and is the spirit of the harvest.

CESAIR, Noah's grand-daughter, brought Ireland's first settlers to Dingle. Some say she is the daughter of Banbha, and arrived 40 days before the Deluge with 50 women, the first sheep and three men. All perished apart from one man, Fionntan.

CROCHAIN CROIDHEARG, daughter of the sun goddess, lives in Oweynagat cave on Crúachan, one of the three sacred caves of Ireland; her name, Blood-Red, refers to sunset, death and gestation.

CROM DUBH or **CROM CRUACH**, the 'bent black' or 'dark croucher', in folk tradition a pagan god who opposes St Patrick. He is antichrist and the devil, a distortion of Dáire and the Daghdha, and often presents Patrick with a cauldron or bullock, after which the saint converts him. Lughnasa often came to be called Crom Dubh's Sunday, with Balar and Lugh's struggle christianised into a confrontation between Patrick and Crom Dubh.

CÚ CHULAINN, mythical hero at the centre of the Ulster Cycle, came from Muirthemhne, Louth and is in some accounts a son of Lugh. The mortally wounded hero tied himself to Cuchulainn's Stone, so as to fight on.

DAGHDHA, the Celtic sun-god. He dwelt in New Grange, impregnated Bóinn to give life to Aonghus. His cauldron left no one unsatisfied and his club either killed or revived those it hit.

DÁIRE, a form of the Daghdha honoured by the Érainn people of Armagh, possessor of a valuable cauldron,

Cil Odhar nr Loch Measca

a fine horse and a great bull. He gave Armagh to St Patrick.

DONN, dark god of the dead, underworld aspect of the Daghdha. He lives in Teach Duinn, Donn's House, on an island in Kenmare Bay. 'To me, to my house, you shall all come.' He brings the dead to his house in Cnoc Fírinne and rides at night on a white horse.

ÉRIU, goddess. Her name, Celtic Iveriu, land, identifies her as a land-goddess. She lies on Uisneach hill, Mídh, the ritual centre of Ireland, her husband is Mac Gréine, 'Son of the sun', representing the ties between female earth and male sun.

FINNBHEARA, the Connacht fairies' leader, presides over a a sídh in Knockmaa hill, his name probably being that of the hilltop cairn. He entices beautiful women into his realm and plays hurling with his fairies against the rest. If they win Connacht's crops flourish.

FIONN MAC CUMHAIL, the famous legendary hero, a warrior-seer, poet and huntsman. He ate the salmon of wisdom, his hood gives him animal form, and he built the Giant's Causeway. His powers, name, poetry and fair hair all derive from an earlier mythological Fionn, a semi-divine seer.

FÍR BOLG brothers, the five sons of Nemhedh, split Ireland between them with its centre at Uisneach hill in Mídh. Defeated by the Tuatha Dé Danann they went to the western edges of Ireland. Their leader Aonghus's stronghold was Dún Aonghusa on the Aran Islands.

FOMHÓIRE, the Fomorians, a ferocious race of hideous giants in the northern and western fringes of Ireland. They represent the dark side of the Indo-European myth of a struggle between a bright, divine race, the Tuatha Dé Danann, and these dark opponents.

GRÁINNE, the sun goddess, ljves in Knockgrean, Cnoc Gráinne, Limerick. Her daughter Crochain Croidhearg lives in Oweynagat cave on Crúachan.

LUGH, the ancient Celtic god Lugus, patron of solemn oaths and the harvest, hence the Lughnasa customs. He slays his maternal grandfather, a myth of Mediterranean origin.

Maeve's Cairn, Sligo

MACHA originally simply meant an area of land, but became synonymous with the Mór Ríoghain, the sovereignty goddess of Ulster. Her tumulus was Emhain Macha, and she had a horse cult, hence the story of the pregnant Macha's race against horses.

MAD SWEENEY, Suibhne, in Kerry legends a seventh century king, whose insanity was cured at Gleann na nGealt; according to lore lunatics from all over Ireland assembled here, to drink from the well and eat watercress.

MANANNÁN, ancestral deity of a maritime tribe, by extension the sea god. He controlled the weather, the Isle of Man was his seat and rushes, watery plants, were sacred to him.

MEADHBH 'the intoxicator' goddess, donor of Tara's sovereignty. Ale and horses are associated with her, she mated with all new kings and inebriated them. Originally she was the Celtic goddess Meduva, and her epithet, leathdhearg, 'half-red', probably refers to kingship contests.

MIDHIR, king of the Tuatha Dé Dannan, lord of the sídh, otherworld dwelling of Brí Leith, Slieve Golry in Longford, and foster father of Aonghus, whom he taughr how to take Brú na Bóinne.

MÍL, or **MÍL EASPAINNE**, fictional Irish ancestor in the Lebor Gabála to explain the biblical genealogical origins of the Irish. His sons defeated the Tuatha Dé Dannan at Sliabh Mís.

MÓR MUMHANN, the sovereignty goddess of Cashel, seat of Munster's kings, originally she was the Érainn people's goddess, but later the conquering Eoghanacht transferred her authority to themselves.

NEMHEDH, third settler in Ireland, he cleared twelve plains for farming and lit the first fire at Uisneach, his wife was the goddess Macha.

NÍL, pharaoh Noah's great-great-grandson, father of Scota. He conveniently ties the Irish genealogies into the biblical records, and gives added significance to the name Niall.

OISÍN, the leading figure of the Fianna epic cycle, son on Fionn mac Cumhaill. In medieval literature he became the proponent of ancient wisdom and poetry, and persuaded Patrick to allow the Fianna into heaven.

PARTHALÁN, second settler of Ireland, landed in Mayo with his wife and three sons. Their retainer Beoil instituted the first guest house, Breá cooked and Malaliach brewed. They brought in cattle, fought the Fomhóire, and their line died out 520 years later in a plague.

SCOTA fictional mother of the earliest settlers in Kerry, and buried at Sliabh Mís. Her name is the feminine of the Latin for the Irish, which derives from a word for a raider and probably originally applied to Irish groups attacking Roman Britain.

SHEELA–NA–GIG, a supernatural female, protector of child-bearing women; folk tradition said she was St Patrick's wife, with her feast day on the 18th of March

TUATHA DÉ DANANN, early settlers with knowledge of metal who became divine beings. The name comes from Toutatés, a Continental Celtic word meaning 'deities of the community'. Their appearance in Irish mythology probably derived from the Celtic invaders referring to old Irish sacred sites as the dwellings of the Toutates.

Dunseverick, Co. Antrim, at the end of a high road from Tara.